TABLE OF CONTENTS

ILLUSTRATIONS

TABLES

INTRODUCTION

People must fight for their law as for their city wall.

– Heraclitus

The word security, in the national sense, seems to provoke frequent redefinition. James L.

Jones, the recent National Security Advisor and retired Marine general, called for redefinition in an

October 2012 address to the "clear thinking of the prairie" in Kansas City, MO.[1] Jessica Tuchman

Matthews, former National Security Council director for Global Affairs, entitled her 1989 *Foreign*

Affairs article, "Redefining Security;" Richard Ullman, the Princeton international affairs professor,

used the same title in his 1983 *International Security* article published by MIT Press. Academics,

practitioners, and organizations often wrestle with and recommend new approaches to security,

especially when wars are drawing to a close. The end of the Cold War provided such a time;

redefinitions abounded through the 1990s and usually reflected particular agendas.[2] With good

reason: how policy makers define security determines national resource flows. Individual nations

spend significant amounts of capital and behave in specific ways to pursue their security.

Not only do nations act individually, they negotiate relationships among themselves

striving to create order and avoid insecurity, the prime human cause of which has been war. The

United Nations (UN) is an example of how nations do this. As an institution, the UN joined the post

Cold War fray to suggest a new approach to security. The 1994 UN *Human Development Report*

introduced the concept of human security. This called on decision makers to make policy for the

individual as security's primary referent. Human security disrupted the community of thinkers and

practitioners because previously, especially during the Cold War, the state had been widely

accepted as primary referent.

---

[1] James L. Jones, "Message to the Next Administration: An Unasked for Response," (Address to the Business Executives for National Security dinner, September 6, 2012).

[2] David Baldwin, "The Concept of Security," from 1997 that listed a number of scholars who either used the word "redefine" or directly implied it in the title of their publication.

The word morphed dramatically right after the century turned. Transnational extremists demonstrated means and capability to shockingly strike states from outside the established order. Improved technologies enabled transnational organized crime (TOC) to increasingly threaten security, whether its referent be the individual or the state. Policy makers invoke "security" to deal with these new century challenges. The first sentence of the United States (U.S.) National Security Council strategy on TOC asserts, "Transnational organized crime (TOC) poses a significant and growing threat to national and international security, with dire implications for public safety, public health, democratic institutions, and economic stability across the globe."[3] Responding to the extremists, in what has become the longest war in U.S. history, a coalition of liberal nations demonstrated enduring global reach with large scale military interventions in Afghanistan and Iraq. Indeed, after state on state military operations ceased in both countries, the narrative for both operations centered on bringing security to Afghans and Iraqis. Now, as the use of force winds down, strategic rebalance to the Pacific ramps up, the Arab Spring sees new seasons, the United States becomes an energy exporter, social media grow, and "global weirding"[4] affects the environment, security redefinitions are again likely to emerge. Depending on how decision makers articulate and practitioners act on security policy, these definitions could take on significant ramifications, internally and externally to the state.

In the midst of these interesting times, questions must be asked. What, then, is security? Why is it important? Who or what provides security? For and from whom or what? What is its relationship with defense? How do war and security affect each other? What is human security and how does it affect policy? Why do national decision makers talk about security so much, especially

---

[3] National Security Council, *Strategy to Combat Organized Transnational Crime*, http://www.whitehouse.gov/administration/eop/nsc/transnational-crime/threat (accessed on March 17, 2013).

[4] Amory Lovins, founder and Chief Scientist, Rocky Mountain Institute, "Opening Remarks: A Day in the Life of Rocky Mountain Institute," an address to National Solutions Council members, July 12, 2011.

in terms of power? If they collectively agree that it is an important concept, how have states designed international systems to create security? How do states actually behave in these systems? Why does security constantly need redefinition? What does security look like in our world now and what will it look like in the coming years? This paper will examine these questions to better understand the concept of security. The goal is to envision the essence of security, characterize the current environment, and anticipate its near term future.

The idea of body politic security has existed throughout human history and geography, expressed in thinking, articulation, and practice. Heraclitus presents a straightforward view from ancient Greece in the subtitle quote, though the word "fight" must be open to interpretation. At the end, this paper intends for the reader to be able to ask high fidelity questions as security appears to change and leaders pronounce "national security." Although politicians often bandy the notion about willy nilly, trying to make it mean what they want at the time, policy makers, scholars, and practitioners must share the term more precisely. The idea serves a critical role, affecting how we as individuals and nations live in this "hot, flat, crowded" world.[5]

Whether it is hot and flat or green and renewed, security in the Western political tradition requires a leviathan, a visible and present force that holds people in awe. Sir Thomas Hobbes coined this idea in his 1651 philosophical treatise on the commonwealth, *The Leviathan,* which proposed the state as a visible and present force to hold its political subjects in awe. The word "awe" might confuse a modern day reader, especially in irreverent times. To address this challenge, this paper suggests that "awe" connote a monopoly on the legitimate use of force. Based on that lens, two types of leviathans will be considered through the rest of the paper. The first has to do with the state level leviathan, who has a monopoly on the legitimate use of force within its territory and governs the behavior of people as they interact with others, both inside and outside the state.

---

[5] Thomas H. Friedman, *The World is Flat* (New York: Farrar, Straus and Giroux, 2005), 37. Friedman's 2006 book which forecasted a hot, flat, and crowded world and advocated U.S. support for a green revolution through which America might renew itself.

The second concerns an international leviathan, created by agreements between nations, an entity above or among the states that might hold sovereigns to account in order to govern their behavior with each other. The 1648 Treaty of Westphalia imagined this second kind, one that envisioned a world order intended to prevent war and pursue peace among nations.

Security, then, began operating on two levels. Each had distinctive characteristics and were kept, for the most part, separate. The first had to do with the relationship between sovereign and subjects and manifested in the political, economic, legal, social, and cultural traditions that Hobbes summed up as a particular "manner of life." This intrastate level enjoyed reasonable success in Europe from the 17th century on, and as states consolidated power, focused and exercised governmental authority over people in their territory. Security's second level reached for world order but its ways and means to legitimately wield force was fraught with delay and discord, lending to the perception of realpolitik, that anarchy prevails in the international realm. Among nations, the leviathan tried to negotiate relationships among sovereigns based on agreed-to principles. History shows these as a series of inadequate leviathans: the Treaty of Westphalia, Congress of Vienna, League of Nations, and the UN. These leviathans have been inadequate for a variety of reasons and this paper does not intend to diagnose this directly. More to the point of this paper, each iteration above attempted to apply lessons of the previous failure to further the notion of an international leviathan.

This necessary but insufficient factor at security's international level has interacted with an integral dynamic: its most powerful members. Ever since the Treaty of Westphalia, states within that particular world order have taken action based on interpretation of the principles of that order. Some agreements enjoyed powerful nations who acted to conserve the established world order; others had their primary powers disagree over purpose and turn their back on collective action. To support the Concert of Europe, France perceived a threat and intervened in 1823 to restore Ferdinand VII to the throne, quashing the liberal constitutional process being instituted in Spain. In 1849, Russia intervened in Austro Hungary in a vain attempt to preserve Europe's Concert and keep the eroding empire from breaking apart. On the other hand, Great Britain with the Congress of Vienna and the United States with the League of Nations turned away from the international leviathan they both played significant roles in creating. Post World War II, the Soviet Union, and the United States agreed on the concept of the UN for international security and took action to the extent they could as the UN tried to establish itself as a *de jure* leviathan. At the same time, the Soviet Union and the United States created *de facto* leviathans in and around themselves, a bi polar power balance and nuclear weaponized world that enforced and stimulated certain behaviors from both sides. The dissolution of the Soviet Union provided an inflection point and offered a significant opportunity to redefine international security. The UN then played the human security card. Meanwhile, the United States became the main superpower, acting on the global stage with or without allies.

This paper converges with human security and behavior of the United States and its allies as a global leviathan. The United States, in the lead of like-minded nations, is behaving as the *de facto* leviathan, along the lines of those originally conceived by Sir Thomas Hobbes. As today's main superpower, the United States and its coalitions have the time, space, scale, and reach to act in support of perceived interests, to pursue a world order in support of liberal ideals. For the moment, these nations can and are acting to enforce liberal ideals, aspects of which are reflected in the notion of human security.

METHODOLOGY

The paper starts with understanding security through political history and the publications of security thinkers since the Cold War. State sovereignty and security as we know them today took form in the mid-17th century. Hobbes merely sparked discussion on the nature of a state. Follow-on political philosophers, e.g. John Locke, Montesquieu, and Jean Jacques Rousseau, contributed vital ideas such as liberty and checks and balances to how a state should be conceived by its people, describing in practical detail how a Western state would be constituted; in general, these philosophers contributed liberalism to political thinking. As a collective, Hobbes and the political thinkers of the Enlightenment informed how European nations modified their states and associated security.

Perhaps an advantage, Thomas Jefferson and cohorts had a clean slate and vast territory. They used these liberal ideas as a departure point for the U.S. Declaration of Independence. From the same fount, participants in the Federal Convention of 1787 designed the structure and dynamics of the U.S. Constitution. These documents and their inherent tensions inform how the United States as a state expresses itself, domestically and internationally. This paper will spotlight U.S. security as representative of Western liberalism, current leader of nations who promote liberalism, and main superpower on the world stage. This review intends to demonstrate how the Western way of life begins with the individual as the actual starting point for its system of values, endowed with rights from and accepting responsibilities toward a political state.

After the political history review, the paper turns to security practitioners and scholars during and after the Cold War. It begins with George Kennan, who contributed fundamentally to the U.S. strategic approach to the coming contest. The Cold War helps us understand the essence of security because both sides of the poles used the word extensively throughout. Its meaning metamorphosed from 1946, with the war just ended, to 1994, the introduction of human security. Security's primary referent began clearly as the state; military power and use of force posed the most obvious means to secure the state. As the years went by, though, discourse began to question military focus to achieve security and the debate began to widen as to how a state achieves security. As the end of the Cold War approached, and other large problems affected people, certitude about the state as primary referent began to slip. By 1994, the UN tied human security with human development and pronounced the following:

> Most people instinctively understand what security means. It means safety from the constant threats of hunger, disease, crime and repression. It also means protection from sudden and hurtful disruptions in the pattern of our daily lives--whether in our homes, in

our jobs, and in our communities or in our environment...In the final analysis, sustainable human development is pro-people, pro-jobs, and pro-nature.[6]

Understanding security from Cold War to post Cold War thinking gives context to our current international political environment. This section ends with a review of the strategic narrative written at the Pentagon by Mr. Y and published by the Woodrow Wilson Center at Princeton; its articulation of U.S. security projects a view of the coming security environment. Overall, this literature review intends to inform our vision of what is ahead, presented later in the paper.

Next, this monograph considers the inadequate leviathans from the Treaty of Westphalia to the UN. The Treaty of Westphalia represents the first modern attempt to design a pattern of relations for "peace and amity"[7] among sovereign states. Westphalia unwittingly created a balance of power in Europe with an international leviathan that would prevent any one nation from dominating others through military conquest. Indeed, one could say that Westphalia's leviathan succeeded at Waterloo. The 1815 Congress of Vienna wittingly established a balance of power to conserve the international system. Vienna's leviathan, along with support from powerful nations within the system, contributed to the Concert of Europe, relative peace and stability on the continent until 1848 and no major conflagrations for almost 100 years. Vienna's inadequacy led to WWI's Treaty of Paris and League of Nations, a new type of international leviathan based on concepts of collective security, shared values, and international law articulated by Woodrow Wilson. Recognized shortfalls of the League contributed strength and presence to our current international system, the international leviathan who struggled for legitimate power as an independent institution while two world superpowers rivaled each other across the globe with incompatible ways of life.

---

[6] United Nations, *Human Development Report Overview* (New York: Oxford University Press, 1994), 3.

[7] Yale Law School, *Treaty of Westphalia: The Avalon Project*, http://avalon.law.yale.edu/17th_century/westphal.asp (accessed January 1-March 25, 2013).

The UN differs significantly from previous international security designs, not the least of which is systematized ideational contributions and participation in discourse among nations. The 1986 UN publication, *Concepts of Security,* reviewed basic worldviews of security, showing that nations basically agreed to disagree on security,[8] giving basis to Buzan's much repeated observation that security is "an essentially contested concept."[9] Moreover, *Concepts of Security* acknowledged the disconnect between the collective security system envisioned in the UN Charter and the limited role the UN was playing in international security. Though it does not say how, the report observes that the gap must be bridged for the UN to fulfill its mission. The 1994 *Human Development Report* did more than just record different viewpoints; it sought to find the mechanism to bridge the gap. It intended to change the way nations think of and act on security by injecting the concept of human security. This section culminates by critically examining human security, comparing and contrasting it to Western notions of the state and security. It will be seen that human security, specifically its focus on the individual, resonates closely with principles from Western liberal political thought. That is, Western notions of security and the state synthesize into what appears to be human security intent: the condition in which individuals live.

Case studies follow the review of international systems. The first considers Jamestown colony showing what the leviathan looked like in a state of nature. That this small body politic survived, surrounded by people groups devoted to its demise and threatened by internal political dysfunction, disease, harsh environmental conditions, and lack of resources presents an historical example of what security intends to achieve. It must be noted that although the British Empire was political sovereign for Jamestown, the *de facto* role of the leviathan was played by the Virginia Company of London during the formative years of Jamestown's existence. The second case study

---

[8] United Nations, *Concepts of Security* (New York, 1986).

[9] Barry Buzan, *People, States, and Fear: An Agenda for International Security Studies in the Post Cold War Era*. 2nd ed. (Boulder, CO: Lynne Rienner Publishers, 2008), 6.

will use the Congress of Vienna as a backdrop to take a closer look at the behavior of Great Britain at the Congress of Verona in 1822 and the conduct of Russia as it intervened to support the emperor of Austria Hungary in 1848. The next case study will be the Helsinki Accords. Many credit this 1975 agreeement between the two world powers as introducing the dynamic that unraveled the Soviet bloc and Union in the late 1980s. The last case study will be U.S. led coalition conduct since the end of the Cold War. Of first interest will be how U.S. leaders articulated an approach and followed through with action in Kosovo during the late 1990s. Second will be Libyan intervention in 2011. Third, U.S. policy and actions to counter the Lord's Resistance Army (LRA) in central Africa will present an ongoing security operation.

The paper concludes by asking a central question: is the current security environment, where the United States and its coalition members are acting as global liberal leviathans, a perishing opportunity for liberal constitutional governments to shape the world system? A militarily ascendant China and Mother Russia, though significantly involved in current world order, are not liberal and/or constitutional governments; or at least the relationship between the individual and the state manifests differently from liberal nations. China and Russia are likely to express their power in different ways than Western governments have such as their Security Council vetoes that have hamstrung UN action in Syria. How will Samuel Huntington's predicted "Clash of Civilizations" affect not only states as leviathans but international security as a global leviathan? To begin, though, we turn to the 17th century.

THE LEVIATHAN, ENLIGHTENMENT AND U.S. MANNER OF LIFE

Czeslaw Milosz, the Nobel laureate from the late 20th century, writes, "Since the seventeenth century we have advanced in losing our sense of hierarchy, which assigns first place to what is simplest."[10] Security as we discuss it today emerged in the 17th century with Sir Thomas

---

[10] [10] Czeslaw Milosz, *Roadside Dog* (New York: Farrar, Straus and Giroux, 1998), 157.

9

Hobbes's philosophical treatise on the state, *The Leviathan*, published in 1651. War's devastating effects catalyzed *The Leviathan*. The English Civil War surrounded Hobbes while the Thirty Year War on the European continent gave distant subject as Hobbes formulated his work. Thick with antiquated expression, *The Leviathan* introduces why human beings would want security from the state and offers suggestions as to how human beings might come together to form a state.

Perfunctory reading of Hobbes cites security as a negative value, meaning the absence of insecurity, a state of war, is the goal of a commonwealth. Without policies, actions, and systems from the leviathan to prevent insecurity, the life of man becomes the oft quoted phrase, "solitary, poore, nasty, brutish, and short." Hobbes noted that war, i. e. insecurity, can be experienced just as easily within a state as it can between states if people are not protected by the leviathan. A deeper reading of Hobbes promotes at least two positive principles of security. The first asserts that a reified state starts from the reality of the individual. Simply put, several persons agree to political bonds to form a group, identifiable from other groups and agree to submit, yielding rights and accepting obligations in concert with others in that same group, to a sovereign authority who becomes the leviathan, the governmental force. A process of common constraint describes these obligations:

> That a man be willing, when others are so too, as farre forth, as for Peace, and defence of himself he shall think it necessary, to lay down this right to all things and be contented with so much liberty against other men, as he would allow other men against himselfe.[11]

People submit to this governmental force for a common "manner of life" in order to secure themselves and their property, positive protection from their state.[12]

---

[11] Thomas Hobbes, *Leviathan or the Matter, Forme, & Power of a Commonwealth, Ecclesiastical and Civill*, (printed for Andrew Crooke at the Green Dragon in St. Paul's Churchyard, 1651), 341.

[12] Ibid., 329 and 395.

The second posit: people are more likely to participate in an economically productive way within such a common manner of life, secured by the state. Hobbes expresses this as a double negative:

> without...security... there is no place for Industry; because the fruit thereof is uncertain; and consequently no Culture of the Earth; no Navigation, nor use of the commodities that may be imported by Sea; no commodious Building; no Instruments of moving, and removing such things as require much force; no Knowledge of the face of the Earth; no account of Time; no Arts; no Letters; no Society; and which is worst of all, continuall feare, and danger of violent death.[13]

In other words, the state not only creates space for fruition of human activities but provides ways, e.g., laws, and means, e.g., roads, etc., for individuals to benefit and secure value from productive labor.

This manner of life must be protected by the state, the Common Power, not only from external threats, "Forraigners," but insiders who act extra-systemically to take what is not theirs, or insecurity:

> The only way to erect such a Common Power, as may be able to defend them from the invasion of Forraigners, and the injuries of one another, and thereby to secure them in such sort, as that by their owne industrie, and by the fruites of the Earth, they may nourish themselves and live contentedly.[14]

Common manner of life in a state suggests values, internal processes of living together, systems through which people within that group cooperate politically, economically, socially, culturally, etc. Overall, Hobbes describes security as a process that arises from particular political bonds of a people group designed to create a state that will secure themselves, their property, what they produce, and how they share it in order to live their manner of life, in protection from outside threats and inside harm to one another. In sum, Hobbes articulated clear and present reason for the why of the state and presented some thoughts as to how the state could become a governmental

---

[13] Ibid., 327.

[14] Ibid., 474.

force. However, the operational approach of forming a state that reflected Western values remained underdeveloped.

John Locke and other political philosophers from the Enlightenment developed operational approaches. Late in the 17th century, John Locke wrote his Second Treatise on Government. Locke agreed with Hobbes' fundamental premise: men, in the state of nature as individuals, are free. However, Locke introduced a critical word, "liberty," and distinguished it from license; further, he pronounced clearly that government requires consent of the governed. Locke also added notions of equality and independence, the ability to act "without asking leave or depending upon the will of any other man."[15] Locke argues that the "reason why men enter into society is the preservation of their property," for "their comfortable, safe, and peaceable living, one amongst another, in a secure enjoyment of their properties, and a greater security against any that are not of it."[16]

Thomas Jefferson incorporated Locke's philosophy into the U.S. Declaration of Independence where the word "security" appears as a synonym for government. A "decent respect to the opinions of mankind" caused Jefferson to explain why the American colonies used force to effect their own security. Beginning with the axiom "all men are created equal" and endowed "with certain inalienable Rights" among which are "the right to Life, Liberty, and the pursuit of Happiness," Jefferson applies Locke's principles of "just powers from the consent of the governed," that governments long established should not be changed for "light and transient causes," but when a "long train of abuses and usurpations, pursuing invariably...a design to reduce them under absolute Despotism, it is their right, it is their duty to throw off such Government, and to provide new Guards for their future security."[17] Jefferson acknowledges the leviathan but one with a

---

[15] Alpheus Thomas Mason, ed., *Free Government in the Making: Readings in American Political Thought*, 3rd ed. (New York: Oxford University Press, 1965), 22.

[16] Ibid., 27.

[17] Ibid., 131.

12

specified character. From Hobbes to Locke to Jefferson, the essence of security appears as

individuals who commonly yield rights to unite in political bonds and agreed-to processes in order

to form a sovereign state that will posit, promote, and protect rights of human liberty that include

life, property, and the pursuit of happiness.

Montesquieu in his *Spirit of Laws* furthers Western understanding of liberty in a state.

> In governments, that is, in societies directed by laws, liberty can consist only in the power of doing what we ought to will, and in not being constrained to do, what we ought not to will...political liberty is to be found only in moderate governments... constant experience shows us, that every man invested with power is apt to abuse it... To prevent this abuse...power should be a check to power...Though all governments have the same general end, which is that of preservation, yet each has another particular object.[18]

After his nod to security or "preservation," Montesquieu holds up the Constitution of

England as the model to promote political liberty. The legislative, executive, judicial branches

constituted that the political liberty of the subject is a "tranquility of mind arising from the opinion

each person has of his safety."[19]

The U.S. Constitutional Convention and subsequent Federalist Papers drew heavily on

Montesquieu's call for balancing leviathan's power to serve the individual. The preamble

introduces what governance and security looks like for that particular body politic:

> We, the People of the United States, in Order to form a more perfect Union, establish Justice, insure domestic Tranquility, provide for the common defence, promote the general Welfare, and *secure* the Blessings of Liberty to ourselves and our Posterity...[italics added by author for emphasis][20]

Checks and balances within the three branches of government, as well as the Bill of Rights,

work together so "one man need not be afraid of another."[21] In its entirety, the U.S. Constitution

expresses to those concerned how the U.S. government secures its manner of life within a particular

---

[18] Ibid., 45.

[19] Ibid., 46.

[20] U.S. Constitution, Preamble.

[21] Mason, 46.

political system, perceived as relatively just by the people within (though they adjust it through relatively civil means and public discourse, e.g. universal suffrage, Martin Luther King and discarding values), of individual rights and responsibilities, laws and liberties. Fischer describes the beginnings of the United States as

> the discovery that people could organize a society on the basis of liberty and freedom, and could actually make it work. The ideas themselves were not new in the world, but for the first time, entire social and political systems were constructed primarily on that foundation.[22]

This Western system provides the individual with rights from and responsibilities to the state in return for security provided by the state, a tacit bargain sealed with citizenship. This is the first level of security, the relationship between the individual and his or her state.

SECURITY THEORY, POLICY, AND PRACTICE AS A WORLD POWER

John Ikenberry observes about this Western way of life, "One of the greatest dramas of world politics over the last two hundred years has been the rise of liberal democratic states to global dominance."[23] It did not do so uncontested. Specifically, in the 20th century both fascism and communism as expressed in the Soviet Union, i.e. Bolshevism, challenged liberal democracy to the degree that required violent and destructive war in the first case. The second case required avoiding war because of one result of Western progress, nuclear weapons.

Before the Soviet Union even demonstrated nuclear weapon capability, the contest between the Soviet way of life and Western liberal democracy was succinctly described by George Kennan. A State Department Foreign Service Officer who worked in the Soviet Union since the 1920s, Kennan explained clearly why the Soviet Union threatened the West in the top secret long telegram of February 1946 and Mr. X article from *Foreign Affairs* in August of 1947. Kennan diagnosed the

---

[22] David Hackett Fischer, *Washington's Crossing* (New York: Oxford University Press, 2004) 5.

[23] G. John Ikenberry, *Liberal Leviathan: The Origins, Crisis, and Transformation of the American World Order* (Princeton: Princeton University Press, 2011), 1.

reality of the situation and prescribed a broad strategic approach to addressing the Soviet Union.

Gaddis describes the long telegram

> It was the geopolitical equivalent of a medical X-ray, penetrating beneath alarming symptoms to yield at first clarity, then comprehension, and finally by implication a course of treatment…The clarity came from Kennan's demonstration…that victory in war and security in peace required different strategies...Comprehension followed…the Soviet Union needed external enemies to justify its internal rule… Diplomacy would be of little use in this situation…Hence, Kennan was saying, Americans could secure their interests by meeting their responsibilities.[24]

Kennan's words reached Washington, D.C. at a propitious time, as the United States was reconsidering its policy toward the Soviet Union and looking to be more realistic in its understanding of Soviet behavior. The Secretary of State, James Byrne, delivered a speech that echoed the long telegram's closing words,

> We will not and we cannot stand aloof…if force or the threat of force is used contrary to the purposes of the [UN] Charter. If we are to be a great power we must act as a great power, not only in order to ensure our own security but in order to preserve the peace of the world.[25]

Further, Kennan portrayed the dual character of the Soviet Union. Ostensibly, the Bolshevists would act officially, observe diplomatic formalities, and participate in international organizations to the degree that those contributed to its interests. Clandestinely, the Bolshevists would work to undermine the influence of major Western powers with penetration and control to, in Kennan's words, "disrupt national self confidence, to hamstring measures of national defense, to increase social and industrial unrest, to stimulate all forms of disunity."[26] Kennan finished his long telegram with, "Finally, we must have courage and self-confidence to cling to our own methods and conceptions of human society,"[27] and his Mr. X article with

---

[24] John Lewis Gaddis, *George F. Kennan: An American Life* (New York: Penguin Press, 2011), 228.

[25] Ibid., 226.

[26] Ibid., 220.

[27] George F. Kennan, Telegram 511, George Washington University,

15

Surely, there was never a fairer test of national quality than this…the thoughtful observer [will not complain but thank Providence] which, by providing the American people with this implacable challenge has made their entire security as a nation dependent on them pulling themselves together and accepting the responsibilities of a moral and political leadership that history plainly intended them to bear.[28]

In this environment, the prime referent for security necessarily became the state. Notice, too, that Kennan calls on American individuals to act together to live their values and secure their state.

Realism dominated political thought and rightly so with a fledgling international leviathan in an anarchic world where military might have just been required. Arnold Wolfers noted the trend of realism when he published "*'National Security' as an Ambiguous Symbol*" in Political Science Quarterly in December 1952.[29] Whereas Kennan's writings came from on the ground experience and offered strategic vision, Wolfers publication took a step back to consider things from a more theoretical perspective. Still, he offered useful strategic vision. Baldwin, writing in 1997, credits Wolfers with the following: "It would be an exaggeration to say that conceptual analysis of security began and ended with Wolfers' article in 1952--but not much of one."[30] For Wolfers, Cold War realism affirmed the state as primary referent rather than "individuals, sub-national groups or mankind as a whole."[31] Wolfers explained the national self acquires values that require protection and a state can choose to have more or less security for those values. Protection implies the power to deter an attack or defeat it; thus, security looked primarily to military power. Wolfers illuminates

---

http://www.gwu.edu/~nsarchiv/coldwar/documents/episode-1/kennan.htm (accessed on 21 March 2013).

[28] Kennan, "Soviet Sources of Conduct," *The History Guide, Lectures on Twentieth Century Europe,*, http://www.historyguide.org/europe/kennan.html (accessed on 21 March 2013).

[29] Arnold Wolfers, "National Security as an Ambiguous Symbol," *Political Science Quarterly*, Volume LXVII, Number 4 (December 1952): 481.

[30] David A. Baldwin, "The Concept of Security," *Review of International Studies* Volume 23 (1997): 8.

[31] Wolfers, 481.

a dialectic between objective security, which measures the absence of threats, and subjective security, which intends to allay fears that national values will be attacked.

This subjective-objective dialectic affects international relations in that achieving greater security becomes a function of the power and opportunity that nations possess to minimize danger by their own policies. Because different nations face different dangers and in different degrees, nations cannot be expected to behave uniformly. Wolfers predicted that a nation would put forth efforts for security that would change with the range of values deemed essential enough to protect and that nations would extend national self via regions of special interest. Theoretically, then, logical spatial extension of the range of values would not stop short of world domination, impossible in the Cold War camps of two military superpowers.[32] This aspect went away with the dissolution of the Soviet Union.

Wolfers sees security as a negative value; that is, being secure is nothing but the absence of the evil of insecurity. Security policy must then strike a balance between its desired ends, the means used, and Morgenthau's moral duty of self preservation. In conclusion, to gain a targeted degree of security, which a nation must pay for with sacrifice of other values, Wolfers strategically recommends power to resist an attack or remove incentive to attack while satisfying legitimate demands of others, citing George Kennan's advice to policymakers of using "self restraint in pursuit of national interest."[33]

"Self-control" is another way of saying that, which came about with the notion of common security in the 1980s. The Palme Commission, named after the Swedish Prime Minister who was assassinated in 1986, advanced the notion of common security. Mutual hostility between the Soviet bloc and the West rose significantly in the late 1970s and early 1980s when the Commission began to meet. It promoted the notion that instead of mutual deterrence, mutual interests should be the

---

[32] Ibid., 489.

[33] Ibid., 497.

basis upon which the two hegemons should behave. In the Commmission's view, security is shared, not zero-sum. Commissioners included Cyrus Vance, the former U.S. Secretary of State, and Georgi Arbatov, the director of the Institute for the United States and Canada in the Soviet Union, among other notable luminaries serving in a private capacity but in what came to be widely known as a "second track diplomacy…Roughly speaking, a left/liberal internationalist worldview prevailed."[34] This thinking among elites, to whom leaders from both hegemons listened, helped broaden the notion of security.

Scholars took note as well to widen the framework of security. International scholar Barry Buzan admits security studies became his vehicle for exploring international relations. His first textbook from 1983, *People, States, and Fear*, anticipated the end of the Cold War. He believed that security studies previously overweighed power, i.e. military, in its analysis. Although showing neorealist tendencies in that he believes "the international political system is an anarchy, which is to say that its principal defining characteristic is the absence of overarching government,"[35] Buzan promotes concepts that would put him mostly in the constructivist camp.[36] The state is primary referent. From that base, though, Buzan articulates three levels and five sectors as analytical tools for security policy makers to consider. The three levels are: individuals, states, and international systems. The five sectors are: Political, Military, Economic, Societal, and Environmental.[37]

---

[34] Geoffrey Wiseman, "The Palme Commission: New Thinking About Security," in *International Commissions and the Power of Ideas*, ed. by Thakur, Ramash and Andrew F. Cooper, and John English (New York: United Nations University Press, 2005), 46-48.

[35] Barry Buzan, *People States and Fear: An Agenda for International Security Studies in the Post Cold War Era. 2nd ed.* (Boulder: Lynne Rienner Publishers, 2008), 146.

[36] Marianne Stone, *Security According to Buzan: A Comprehensive Security Analysis*, Security Discussion Papers Series 1 Groupe d'Etudes et d'Expertise "Sécurite et Technologies" (GEEST) (Spring, 2009): 2.

[37] Barry Buzan, "New Patterns of Global Security in the Twenty First Century," *International Affairs*, 67.3 (1991): 433.

Moreover, he recognizes the role of regional nations who form relational security phenomena through amity via shared interests, e.g. NATO, or enmity, e.g. Israel.[38]

Central also to Buzan is the character of a particular state, which can be triangularized into components: its idea, its physical base, and its institutional expression, reproduced below. The Declaration of Independence and U.S. Constitution form examples of what Buzan is referring to as a nation's idea.[39]

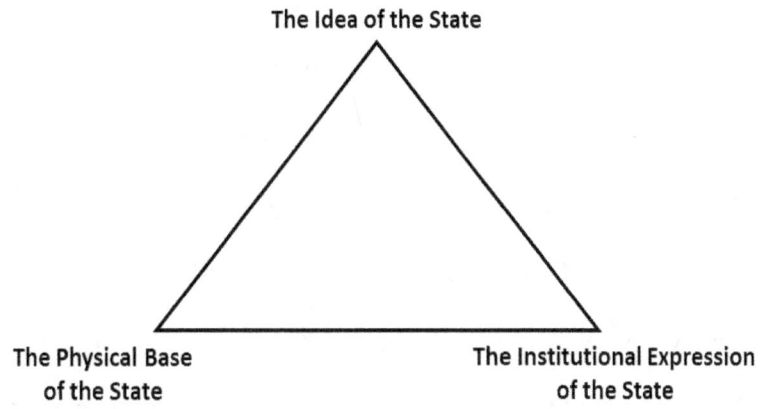

Figure 1. Buzan's Character of State

These connect to and interact with that state's individuals at micro levels of, say, life, health, status, wealth, and freedom. Moreover, that state expresses itself institutionally via foreign policy and actions on the world stage. Buzan's "national security problematique" as an "essentially contested concept,"[40] arises from his suggestion that understanding security comes from examining the complex linkages between these micro level factors, the state in which they exist, and the macro

---

[38] Stone, 6.

[39] Buzan, *People, States, and Fear*, 65.

[40] An essentially contested concept has a specific definition according to W. B. Gallie. It must be "appraisive in the sense that it signifies or accredits some kind of valued achievement." See Baldwin, "The Concept of Security," 1997 for a more developed explanation.

systems in which those states operate.[41] Buzan prescribes that a state's security policy not only consider outward or international dynamics but inward or intranational factors and mix the two in accordance with how policymakers perceive threats and vulnerabilities.[42] In sum, Buzan broadens Wolfers' view with, "The bottom line of security is survival but it also reasonably includes a substantial range of concerns about the conditions of existence,"[43] the three levels, five sectors, and relational phenomena.

Buzan was not alone in broadening security in the early 1980s. Northern Europeans such as Johan Galtung and Jan Øberg formulated an alternative security concept based on four sets of positive goals related to human needs: survival, development, freedom, and identity.[44] Further, a colleague of Buzan's, Ole Weaver, refined the idea by focusing on the use of the word security as a "speech act." With primary referent still the state, Weaver promoted the notion that nations securitize, i.e. make an issue a security concern, through a process whereby elites declare an issue to be a national security problem. The word should have specific and serious meaning; when invoked, a state official can claim a special right to use whatever means necessary to block a threat.[45]

Weaver affirms being responsible with the word, rejects the notion of the masses in determining security, and suggests seeing fewer factors as security threats, or desecuritizing, as valuable:

> That elites frequently present their interests in "national security" dress is, of course, often pointed out by observers...Their actions are then labelled something else, for example,

---

[41] Buzan, *People, States, and Fear*, 65.

[42] Stone, 7.

[43] Buzan, *New Patterns of Global Security in the Twenty-first Century*, 433.

[44] Ole Weaver, Securitization, and Desecuritization, *On Security*, ed. Ronnie D. Lipschutz (New York: Columbia University Press, 1995), 48.

[45] Ibid., 55.

"class interests," which seems to imply that authentic security is, somehow definable independent of elites, by direct reference to the "people." This is, in a word, wrong. Security is articulated only from a specific place, in an institutional voice, by elites. All of this can be analyzed, if we simply give up the assumption that security is, necessarily, a positive phenomenon.[46]

Later in the paper, the Helsinki Accords case study will combine Weaver's prescription with the strategic vision of Kennan and Wolfers as a way of understanding how the West remained standing and the Soviet Union dissolved after the Cold War.

Human security emerged after the Cold War. Emma Rothschild titled her 1995 publication, "What is Security?" partly in an attempt to put human security into historical and political context. She began with

> Principles or definitions of security are a well established institution of international politics. They are of great importance, in particular, to the ceremonials of reconstruction after large international wars.[47]

She noted the aftermath of the Cold War as no different and took particular notice of common security and human security, which she construed as "security of individuals as an object of international policy." To Rothschild, these notions were not particularly new and could be easily found in Kantian liberalism. Furthermore, Leibniz wrote in 1705 defining the state as a "great society of which the object is common security ('la seureté commune')." Montesquieu included security in his definition of both the state and freedom. Rousseau described the social contract as the outcome of individuals' desire for security of life and liberty: "this is the fundamental problem to which the institution of the state provides the solution." Rothschild answers her title question with security is a "condition, or an objective, that constitute[s] a relationship between individuals

---

[46] Ibid., 57.

[47] Emma Rothschild, "What is Security?" *Daedalus* 124, 3 (Summer 1995): 53.

and states or societies."[48] Rothschild, as will be explained in the section on human security, appears skeptical of common and human security as objects of international policy.

David Baldwin followed Rothschild in exploring the concept of security in 1997. However, Baldwin approached the concept quite differently. His aim was to identify common and fundamental conceptual distinctions to the different conceptions of security for social science scholars to communicate more effectively with each other and for rational policy analysis. Baldwin refutes Buzan's suggestion that security is an "essentially contested concept," which would require it to be an appraisive concept, make conceptual analysis futile, and make the goal of correct or standard use of the word improbable. Baldwin argues that security is inadequately explicated.[49]

The state remains primary referent for Baldwin though he suggests his analysis is applicable to any level or entity: individual, family, society, state, international system, or humanity. As mentioned previously, Baldwin considers Wolfers to have provided the most sound basis to discuss security as a concept but reformulates the point of departure, Wolfers's negative value, from "the absence of threats to acquired values" to "a low probability of damage to acquired values" to focus the concept on preservation of acquired values.[50]

Baldwin identifies two simple specifications to define how the word is used:

- *Security for whom?*
- *For which values?*

The above specifications merely help define how the word is used. Baldwin offers further questions to make alternative security policies comparable and help guide policy makers:

---

[48] Rothschild, 61-4.

[49] Baldwin discusses essential contestedness at length then refers to W. B. Gallie's appraisive definition and following counterarguments. See W. B. Gallie, "Essentially Contested Concepts," *Proceedings of the Aristotelian Society*, N. S., 56 (1956):167-98, and Christine Swanton, "On the 'Essential Contestedness' of Political Concepts," *Ethics*, 84 (1973): 811-27.

[50] Baldwin, 13.

- *How much security?* Security becomes a matter of degree, absolute security being

    unattainable.

- *From what threats?* This allows entities to perceive based on their situation, e.g.

    ideological, economic, military, environmental.

- *By what means?* A nation can pursue security through a variety of means.

- *At what cost?* This accounts for cost of a particular security policy.

- *In what time period?* Time horizon affects proper action.[51]

Baldwin endorses the marginal value approach as a process for valuing security. Besides being long advocated by defense economists, this approach offers the best solution to resource allocation problems, recognizing security as only one of many policy objectives competing for scarce resources. Baldwin criticizes Buzan and, by implication, Weaver here; Baldwin construes their writings to prejudge the importance of security.[52]

Noting the disagreement highlights an important distinction between considered theorists. Baldwin and Wolfers are engaged in a more theoretical and conceptual discussion of security. Whereas the collective of Hobbes plus Locke et al, Buzan, Weaver, and Rothschild engage in more operationalizable discussions of state security.[53] Hobbes, Locke et al, speak of security and refer not only to the state and its power but to the conditions in which individuals live. In this sense, the whole of state policies, intranational and international, determine conditions in which people live, the manner of life.

Baldwin perceives overemphasis on the military in thinking about security:

During the Cold War, security studies was composed mostly of scholars interested in military statecraft. If military force was relevant to an issue, it was considered a security

---

[51] Ibid., 12-18.

[52] Ibid., 19-21.

[53] For more on this distinction, see Robert A. Dahl, "The Concept of Power," *Behavioural Science,* 2 (1957). Dahl stages a dialogue between a theoretical conceptualist and an operationalist.

issue...if military force was not relevant, that issue was consigned to the category of low politics...military force, not security, has been the central concern of security studies.[54]

Baldwin suggests the aim should be for value neutral policy analysis: how discrete policies, some devoted to security, others to education, others to taxation might be evaluated one against the other. In other words, Baldwin is more interested in the theoretical concept of entity security as a policy in an intrinsically insecure space while the other theorists point to practical security in a manner of life among mortal individuals in a world of states that exist in a mostly anarchic environment.

Baldwin concludes by asserting that his concept of security implies nothing whatsoever about the degree of interdependence among states with respect to their security relations. That is, Baldwin addresses coalition security with his question Security for whom? cited in an empirical investigation, not built into the definition of security.[55] Thereby, Baldwin again differentiates his work from that of Buzan, Weaver, and Rothschild, who note the tendency of states in history to form international arrangements for security.

Baldwin updated Wolfers's 1952 conceptual security article into the post Cold War world. Mr Y did the same thing for the Mr. X article. That is, for practical security, nothing demonstrates the delta for security thought in the United States better than comparing Kennan's 1947 Mr. X article and the Mr. Y strategic narrative published in 2011 by the Woodrow Wilson Center at Princeton. In 2009, Admiral Mike Mullen, the Chairman of the Joint Chiefs of Staff, charged Captain Wayne Porter, U.S. Navy, with writing a U.S. grand strategy. CAPT Porter joined forces with Colonel Mark Mykleby, USMC, and composed a 15-page intellectual framework to inspire and guide U.S. government agencies entitled, A National Strategic Narrative. Dr. Anne-Marie Slaughter from Princeton summarizes this 21st century narrative into one sentence:

---

[54] Ibid., 9.

[55] Ibid., 26.

24

We [the U.S.] want to become the strongest competitor and most influential player in a deeply inter-connected global system, which requires that we invest less in defense and more in sustainable prosperity and the tools of effective global engagement.[56]

Slaughter distinguishes Mr. Y from Mr. X, pointing out that Kennan's narrative highlighted U.S. leadership of the free world against the communist world where the United States would "invest in containing the Soviet Union…limiting its expansion while building a dynamic economy and as just, and prosperous a society as possible."[57] Mr. Y prescribes the following five thought process transitions for the United States from the Cold War to the current and coming security environment.[58]

Table 1. Mr. Y's Thought Process Transitions

From	To
control in a closed system	credible influence in an open system
containment	sustainment
deterrence and defense	civilian engagement and competition
zero sum global politics/economics	positive sum global politics/economics
national security	national security and prosperity

The table below summarizes the previous two sections of this paper.

Table 2. Comparison of Theories As They Relate to Security

Theorist	Referent	International Relations Theory	Characteristic Phrase on Security	Theoretical or Practical
Mr. X	state	realist	• contain Soviets • live U.S. values	practical

---

[56] Anne-Marie Slaughter, Preface to *A National Strategic Narrative BY: Mr. Y*, http://www.wilsoncenter.org/sites/default/files/A%20National%20Strategic%20Narrative.pdf, page 3 (accessed on 24 March 2013).

[57] Ibid., 2.

[58] Ibid., 3-4.

Theorist	Referent	International Relations Theory	Characteristic Phrase on Security	Theoretical or Practical
Wolfers	state	realist	• protect acquired values of national self	theoretical
Buzan	state	constructivist/ neorealist	• essentially contested • conditions of existence	practical
Weaver	state	constructivist	• speech act	practical
Rothschild	state	realist	• relationship between state and individual	practical
Baldwin	state but applicable to any level	not identifiable	• inadequately explicated	theoretical
Hobbes alone	state	realist	• The Leviathan • Commonwealth • manner of life	practical
Hobbes+ Locke et al	state + individual	realist + liberal	• rights, life, liberty, property, pursue happiness	practical
Mr. Y	state + individual	realist constructivist	• open system • sustainment • competition • positive sum • prosperity	practical

Western liberal ideas on security converge into a relationship between individuals and the leviathan, state governance systems, that bring about, enforce, and protect a valued way of life. Security, then, becomes a process of selecting, protecting, sustaining, and letting go of values as articulated by leaders and acted on by operators in service to the people in that particular body politic. By implication, people require right reasons to hold their leviathan in awe. As will be seen at the end of the next section, human security represents the current international leviathan's proposal to guide member states' leaders and policy makers on the nature of the relationship between government and its people.

INADEQUATE LEVIATHANS: INTERNATIONAL ORDERS SINCE WESTPHALIA

So far, this paper has suggested that Western concepts point to a first level of security: the relationship between individuals and their state. A second level appears as to how Western nations coalesce around the notion of security. The Treaty of Westphalia represents the first attempt of modern Western nations to strive for security as a group. This treaty, which was a series of agreements with the last one signed in 1648, urgently sought to end the Thirty Years War. The first paragraph expresses intent to achieve peace and promote friendship among signatory nations.

> [The parties] have form'd Thoughts of an universal Peace...there shall be a Christian and Universal Peace, and a perpetual, true, and sincere Amity... that thus on all sides they may see this Peace and Friendship in the Roman Empire...by entertaining a good and faithful Neighbourhood.[59]

France, Spain, Austro-Hungary, the Dutch Republic, Denmark, Sweden, England, and a series of German protestant princes signed the treaty.

Just as important as the strategic goals of peace and amity was the how of achieving them. Key operating principles designed into the treaty of Westphalia consolidated the concept of territorial states and established this 17th century international system. Principles included general recognition of exclusive sovereignty, rights and responsibilities of each party over its land, people, and agents abroad, and the doctrine of *cuius regio, eius religio,* (each region, its religion) which commonly stipulated among the parties that each sovereign had the power to determine that region's dominant belief system. As an important nod to religious freedom, Christians were guaranteed the right to practice their individual belief system in private or during allotted hours when their belief system was not the dominant denomination.[60]

At the same time semi sacrosanct sovereignty established order and solved immediate problems, it injected an unpredictable dynamic into Europe: *raison d'etat,* or national interest. Cardinal Richelieu, the 17th century French statesman, gave the term historical life. For internal

---

[59] Treaty of Westphalia, http://avalon.law.yale.edu/17th_century/westphal.asp (accessed on 21 March 2013).

[60] See Barro, R. J. and McCleary, R. M. "Which Countries Have State Religions?" *Quarterly Journal of Economics*, Volume 120, Number 4 (2005): 1334. With the Peace of Westphalia, the member states agreed to respect private worship, liberty of conscience, and rights of migration for religious minorities within their domains.

security, Richelieu consolidated French royal power, ruthlessly eliminated rival authorities, and centralized France. With regard to external security, he delayed German unification by about two centuries and thereby reduced threats from the east. Richelieu believed, "In matters of state, he who has the power often has the right, and he who is weak can only with difficulty keep from being wrong in the opinion of the majority of the world."[61] Indeed, Richelieu's raison d'etat became a guiding principle of European international relations. States pursued power and acted on policies whose success depended mostly on the ability to assess power relationships.[62] (In an aside, and perhaps illustrative as to why the United Kingdom often chooses to separate itself from the European continent, one might contrast Richelieu's statement with a narrative created by England's King Arthur mythology, "Might does not make right. Right makes might.")

Initially, and for almost 150 years, a balance of power was established in Europe.[63] A balance of power is meant to limit the ability of states to dominate others and, if war does break out, limit its scope. As far as peace was concerned, though, the Treaty of Westphalia failed immediately and repeatedly. France and Spain remained at war until 1659. Frederick the Great wielded Prussian armies to carve territory into his kingdom throughout the first half of the 18th Century. France and Great Britain fought each other frequently both in Europe and via their colonies. However, no nation came to dominate; wars between major powers remained relatively limited. The goal of balance of power is stability. However, it cannot satisfy every member of the international system completely. Kissinger points out, "[balance of power] works best when it keeps dissatisfaction below the level at which [an] aggrieved party will seek to overthrow the international order."[64]

---

[61] Henry Kissinger, *Diplomacy* (New York: Simon & Schuster, 1994), 65.

[62] Ibid., 63.

[63] Carl Von Clausewitz, *On War*, ed. and trans by Michael Howard and Peter Paret (Princeton: Princeton University Press, 1984), 590.

[64] Kissinger, 21.

Kissinger refers to balance of power in general. Clausewitz explains specifically what happened to interstate order over the course of the 18th century.

> The conduct of war thus became a true game...a more forceful method of negotiation...It had ceased to be in harmony with the spirit of the times to plunder and lay waste the enemy's land...Armies came to form a state within a state, in which violence gradually faded away. All Europe rejoiced...this development benefited the peoples of Europe.[65]

This happy order did not persist. Liberal ideas, so essential to the founding of the United States, translated into clenched fists, shouts of *liberté, egalité, e fraternité,* and regicide in France, vigorously capable of spreading via state policy and action. Clausewitz tells us these revolutionary ideas set about destroying the conservative European order.

> ...in 1793 a force appeared that beggared all imagination...Suddenly, war again became the business of the people, a people of thirty millions...The revolutionary quarrels did not yet advance toward the ultimate conclusion: the destruction of the European monarchies...due to technical imperfections...Once these imperfections were corrected by Bonaparte, this juggernaut of war, based on the strength of the entire people, began its pulverizing course through Europe...War had broken loose in all its elemental fury...Will this always be the case in future?[66]

Besides a presage of World Wars I and II, Clausewitz points to security being shattered when a nation breaks loose in a radical way from what was the accepted international order. It must be pointed out, though, even when France rejected peace and amity and turned to conquest, the Treaty of Westphalia achieved its overall intent at Waterloo. What price, success?

To restore Europe in 1815, policy makers turned to what the Treaty of Westphalia effected and what conserved their way of life before Napoleon: balance of power. The Congress of Vienna drew on William Pitt's plan and designed equilibrium into the international system through national power; it also called to a limited degree on a sense of shared values and justice, a moral dynamic among the signatory states. Territorial rebalancing, to include French concerns even as a defeated foe, and consolidation (but not unification) of Germany addressed physical interests. Castlereagh,

---

[65] Clausewitz, 590-1.

[66] Ibid., 592-3.

the British representative, recognized that France theoretically had the power to dismember Europe but the "moral force which can alone hold such a confederacy together" would bind the Quadruple Alliance (Austria, Russia, Prussia, and Great Britain) to counter French power. Moreover, Austria's Metternich induced principle signatories to submit disagreements to a sense of shared values, principles of restraint.[67] Thus, the Congress of Vienna continued to hold meetings over the following decades at a variety of stately locations; this period came to be known as the Concert of Europe.

Concert it may have been from an ivory tower. Considered from the grass roots, though, discord sounded seven years later. Cacophony broke out in 1848 and the Crimean War scattered the players in 1854, inasmuch as Europe avoided massive war until WW I. In 1822, representatives from the Quadruple Alliance plus France (which had been restored to inclusion as a major power) met in Verona to consider liberal and revolutionary developments in Spain. France wanted conservative unity – endorsement – for its intended action to intervene and restore Ferdinand the VII as monarch in Spain. Great Britain, represented by Lord Wellington, opposed. Castlereagh articulated why in 1820. The Quadruple Alliance came together for the

> liberation of a great proportion of the continent from the military dominion of France...It never was, however, intended as an Union for the Government of the World or for the Superintendence of the Internal Affairs of other States.[68]

Great Britain, arguably the most formidable power in Europe, rejected the notion of an international order able to intervene in a state's governmental affairs to secure itself. France intervened with concurrence from the remaining three powers, dashed Spanish liberal constitutionalism and re-imposed the harmony it wanted to hear at the leviathan level. Russia also intervened to conserve this second tier leviathan for European order in 1848. Tsar Nicoloas I sent 200,000 troops to reverse the Austro-Hungarian revolution. Both French and Russian interventions

---

[67] Kissinger, 79-82.

[68] Ibid., 91.

kept the international leviathan intact and prevented individuals within those states from renegotiating their relationships with their state. More will be discussed on this point in the case study section of the paper. The Crimean War disbanded the Concert of Europe. The several nations returned to limited conflict at times, building power in the balance all the while, especially Prussia under Bismarck, viz, Germany.

The next explicit international order did not pursue balance of power. In fact, U.S. President Woodrow Wilson believed power balance induced states to comport toward eventual explosive destruction of international order, the evil of insecurity. Instead, after WWI, Wilson proposed to base peace as a legal concept on the principle of collective security, which would require an international institution, the League of Nations. Moreover, whereas European powers previously redrew state boundaries to preserve power balance with little to no regard for individual choice for body politic, Wilson saw peoples' right to self determination as indispensable to collective security arrangements. In Wilson's own words, "[N]o nation should seek to extend its polity over any other nation or people... [A]ll nations [should] henceforth avoid entangling alliances which would draw them into competitions of power."[69]

Wilson's plan, the League of Nations, was quickly experienced as inadequate. However, Wilson's idealism affected how the United States came to approach world order throughout the 20th century. In a speech before the Senate in 1917 Wilson proposed that equal rights among states supported peace through collective security.

> Right must be based upon the common strength, not upon individual strength, of the nations upon whose concert peace will depend...no one asks or expects anything more than an equality of rights. Mankind is looking now for freedom of life...[70]

---

[69] Kissinger, 222-4.

[70] Woodrow Wilson, An Address to Senate, January 22, 1917, http://www.firstworldwar.com/source/peacewithoutvictory.htm (accessed on February 24, 2013).

Kissinger sees similarities between Castlereagh, the British foreign minister at the Congress of Vienna, and Wilson. Both had genuine interest in general peace. Both thought the best way to pursue that interest was to participate in shaping decisions affecting international order and in countering violations to that peace. At the same time, Kissinger notes the weakness of collective security: interests are rarely uniform and security is rarely seamless. Therefore, members of such an arrangement tend to agree on inaction rather than joint action or they may see the most powerful member extract itself because that nation needs that system least.[71] The League of Nations lasted 27 years, with spotty participation. The United States neither ratified the Treaty of Versailles nor joined the League of Nations. However, it metamorphosed into the UN following WWII.

The first two purposes of the UN Charter echo the "Peace" and "Amity" of the Treaty of Westphalia.

> 1. To maintain international peace and security, and to that end: to take effective collective measures for the prevention and removal of threats to the peace, and for the suppression of acts of aggression or other breaches of the peace, and to bring about by peaceful means, and in conformity with the principles of justice and international law...

> 2. To develop friendly relations among nations based on respect for the principle of equal rights and self-determination of peoples, and to take other appropriate measures to strengthen universal peace;

Note these purposes call on shared values, principles of justice and international law, elements of Wilson's original articulation for an international institution. Article 1, from which the above come, also presents third and fourth purposes: to achieve economic, social, cultural, and humanitarian international cooperation and to harmonize the actions of nations in attaining these common ends. The notions of shared values, international law, cooperation, and harmonization diminish appearance of power balance schemes that gave structure to previous international orders. Having said that, power balance did *de facto* play an important role in world order during the Cold War.

---

[71] Kissinger, 90-1.

That power balance played out in Great Power aggression, for which the UN proved ineffective. However, the UN provided a useful forum for the exchange of ideas.[72] In 1986, the Department for Disarmament Affairs of the Secretary General of the UN under Javier Perez de Cuellar published Concepts of Security. This document unmistakably reads the state as primary referent. The introduction posits and conclusion reiterates

> In principle, security is a condition in which States consider that there is no danger of military attack, political pressure or economic coercion, to that they are able to pursue freely their own development and progress. International security is thus the result and the sum of the security of each and every State member of the international community...security is a relative rather than an absolute term. National and international security need to be viewed as matters of degree.[73]

The report represents UN efforts to referee the Cold War world. It provides an overview of security concepts, identifies problems and threats in international security, prescribes measures to promote international peace and security, and offers conclusions and recommendations to encourage national policy makers to "look into the problem in its entirety."[74] More specifically, the problem identified security as comprehensive in a more interdependent age, neither divisible in its military, economic, social and political dimensions nor between its national and international aspects.

Especially cognizant, and doubting the effectiveness, of military power in an arms race with weapons of mass destruction, the report highlights the quandary that non aligned, developing, and smaller states had with regard to security. In doing so, the report only makes one reference to individuals, pointing out that security is conceived at the most basic level in the struggle for individual survival for many of the four billion inhabitants in developing countries. Importantly, among perfunctory remarks in the Measures to Promote International Peace and Security, the report

---

[72] Ibid., 249.

[73] United Nations, *Concepts of Security*, 2.

[74] Ibid., 3.

makes a profound admission about a disconnect between the collective security system envisioned in the UN Charter and the limited role the UN was playing in international security. Though it does not say how, the report observes that the gap must be bridged for the UN to fulfill its role.[75] The end of the Cold War may have allowed the UN a proposal to fill that gap.

The 1994 UN Human Development Report proposed human security. The first sentence states, "The world can never be at peace unless people have security in their daily lives."[76] Indeed, the report sets forth a number of radical ideas: a new world social charter, a compact to implement targets for essential human development, spending monies that flowed from the end of the Cold War as a peace dividend on development, a global human security fund, a more robust UN to administer human development, and an Economic Security Council.[77] The report believes "for too long" potential for conflict, territorial threats, and weapons have defined elements of or have been ways to protect security.

The Human Security chart that corresponds with previous theorists appears as:

Table 3. Human Security as a Theory

Theorist	Referent	Theory	Phrase	Practical Theoretical
Human Security	Individual	Liberalism	Human Development	Both

A previously considered theorist, Rothschild, sees human security as a refrain from history.

The two principal constituents of "human security or "common security" in the 1990s…were also the preoccupations of late Enlightenment liberalism…the human rights of 1948 are also the rights of the American and French Revolutions…described as "the natural rights of humanity." These rights begin with "the security of one's person, a security which includes the assurance that one will not be troubled by violence…within

---

[75] Ibid., 23.

[76] United Nations, *Human Development Report*, 1.

[77] Ibid., 3-11.

34

one's family or in the use of one's faculties," and proceed, through the security and free enjoyment of one's property," to the right of political participation.[78]

At the same time, Rothschild considers shortcomings of human security. Among them is the "dizzying" geometric complexity of inclusiveness, which causes psychological and political incoherence. Moreover, a nebulous set of rights from a remote institution does not follow liberal political theory; individuals must be conscious of and understand their rights in a body politic. Interposing rights from the international realm can be insidious and subvert a more local and flexible political process, which may be the most sustainable source of security. Rothschild suggests, though, human security will be a continuing political feature of the post-Cold War period and an effort to make sense of this idea is of continuing importance.[79]

MacFarlane and Khong do just that in 2006. As an installment in the UN Intellectual History Project Series, they critically examine the history of human security and the UN. MacFarlane and Khong present arguments that revolve around the UN's significant role in creating ideational change regarding security within and among nations. The UN not only provided a forum to question the primacy of the state in security during the Cold War, it proposed and cultivated human security. UN bodies used what authority they had to define new norms for sovereignty and state responsibility. Moreover, epistemic networks from the UN disseminated understanding of, and promoted, human security throughout national bureaucracies. UN agencies then became active in implementing the concept in their field programs.[80]

Whereas some nations have embraced human security, others have not. Canada, Japan, Norway, and Switzerland have used it in decisions allocating resources; such application has evolved the concept. Other states actively resist the replacement or supplementing of state security.

---

[78] Rothschild, 67.

[79] Ibid., 70.

[80] S. Neil MacFarlane and Yuen Foong Khong, *Human Security and the UN: A Critical History* (Indianapolis: Indiana University Press, 2006), 9.

This second group of states perceive potential challenge to state prerogatives. MacFarlane and Khoong point to the United States, Russia, and China as appearing in the second group and, as a result, are not surprised that Security Council resolutions have not used the term human security. Having said that, though, major UN related commissions (the International Commission on Intervention and State Sovereignty, the Commission on Human Security, and the High level Panel on Threats, Challenges, and Change) present human security as a central tenet in understanding security issues.[81]

MacFarlane and Khoong make important conclusions. The very debate engendered by human security has moved more weight toward the individual and away from the state as primary referent for security; this follows a highly regarded maxim articulated well by Vaclav Havel, "Our policies—foreign and domestic—must grow out of ideas, above all out of the idea of human rights"[82] However, MacFarlane and Khoong see serious problems in characterizing security in economic, environmental, health, and other terms. Conflating human development with security creates conceptual confusion, has not produced nor is it likely to bring about greater access to resources, distracts from the underemphasized problem of violence, and might even encourage military solutions to social and economic problems. Indeed, qualifying sovereignty on human development terms could have the unintended effect of weakening the principle of non-intervention, and in turn, produce more disorder and suffering.

MacFarlane and Khoong recommend a more restrictive notion of human security, one constrained to protecting human beings from threats of organized violence. This approach makes it less probable to transcend or marginalize the state in its role of protecting the people. At the same time it introduces a qualification for sovereignty: compliance with international expectations regarding the protection of human beings. MacFarlane and Khoong finish their study by noting

---

[81] Ibid., 10.

[82] Rothschild, 66.

differences in the relationship between a state and its citizens from the two most recent turns of the centuries. Whereas in 1900 there was no qualification for sovereignty in how a state related to its citizens, no international interest in the rights of women and children affected by conflict, no question about the acceptability of recruiting children to fight wars, no meaningful consideration of non military matters as aspects of security, now there is. Furthermore, whereas there was no consensus on legitimacy or acceptability of intervention in states when they systematically persecute their citizens, now a consensus has emerged. (The situation in Libya from 2010 demonstrates this and will be considered later in the paper.) The evolution that has taken place with human security has been a substantial accretion of norms and a normative framework for the international protection of human beings and holding to account states that fail this responsibility. This framework is "likely (imperfectly) to deter...abuse" of people.[83]

CASE STUDIES

The first two sections of this paper reviewed political history and security theory. The second section examined how states organize around the concept of international security and culminated in better understanding the UN notion of human security. Next, this paper will consider case studies to examine how humans and nations have behaved with regard to security. The first will study the colony of Jamestown on the North American continent. The next will look at the behavior of nations after the Congress of Vienna. The third will observe the effect of the Helsinki Accords on the Soviet Union. The fourth considers U.S. actions on the world stage as the sole superpower after the Cold War.

Jamestown shows in microcosm why security matters and how a body politic endured. Similar settlements did not, e.g. Roanoke, Ajacan, Fort Caroline, and Sable Island. Surrounded by people groups committed to destroy the site and its inhabitants, threatened by starvation, lack of

---

[83] MacFarlane and Khoong, 11-18 and 261-270.

supplies, a harsh environment, disease, and political infighting, Jamestown survived, often just.

King James I granted the Virginia Company of London a charter to establish a colony in June 1606,

which made the company, in effect, the first level leviathan for the ensuing 17 years. The initial

group of men and boys arrived in North America in May 1607. Written orders, not opened until

arrival, instructed the colonists to establish an inland settlement to avoid exposure to England's

ocean going European enemies. Those orders also selected Captain John Smith as a member of the

governing council, though he had been scheduled to be hanged for perceived transgressions on the

trans Atlantic voyage.

Captain Smith played a critical role in the next two years of Jamestown's survival,

reconnoitering, leading the use of force in offensive and defensive operations against the natives,

and trading with them for food. An injury forced Smith to return to England for medical treatment,

which coincided with the settlement's Starving Time, from October 1609 to June 1610. Only 60 of

214 people survived and were abandoning Jamestown when a supply ship arrived not only with

required sustenance but a new governor, Thomas West, Baron de LaWarre. The following year

brought more supplies from the Virginia Company with a deputy governor, Sir Thomas Dale, "the

first man in authority to see what was wrong."[84] Dale has been credited by history for instituting a

strict penal code into the colony. However, according to Bethell, Dale's more important

contribution was quickly changing Jamestown rules to introduce private property. For an opinion

from the time, Ralph Hamor wrote in *The True Discourse of the Present Estate of Virginia* in 1615,

> Sir Thomas Dale hath taken a new course throughout the whole colonie…he hath allotted
> to every man in the colonie, three English acres of cleere Corne ground, which every man
> is to mature and tend…and they are not called unto any service or labour belonging to the
> Colonie, more than one month in a yeere, for which, doing no other dutie to the Colonie,
> they are yeerely to pay into the store two barrels and a halfe of Corne…[85]

---

[84] Tom Bethell, *The Noblest Triumph: Property and Prosperity Through the Ages* (New York: St. Martin's Press, 1998), 34.

[85] Ibid., 35

Bethell also points to minimal taxation in the above as adding to individual incentive.[86] Productivity at the micro level turned around and reversed the pattern of settlers having to rely on Indians for corn. Dale turned the economic system to the individual and brought in rules that governed the community until 1619, when the first House of Burgesses convened as the first democratically elected legislature in America.[87]

The first item on the 1619 Burgess agenda was a shared economic concern: the price of tobacco. Having addressed the issue of hunger through private property, the colony also began producing tobacco. Nine years previous, arriving on one of the makeshift ships cobbled together in Bermuda after the sinking of one of the Virginia Company supply ships, Sir John Rolfe brought with him the seeds, literally, of Jamestown's early economic toe hold. Nicotiana tabacum, a strain that Rolfe found in Bermuda as a result of the shipwreck, appealed to European taste much more than the tobacco cultivated in Jamestown previously. By 1612, Rolfe was exporting with profit. Other community members followed suit and by 1617 Jamestown produced 50,000 pounds of tobacco for export, enough content for an economically viable enterprise.[88]

Economic content only would be insufficient. People must have economic systems based on rules into which they invest themselves for a way of life that endures. The leviathan, Virginia Company, achieved this with what was called Hundreds, through which financial investors in London sent shiploads of settlers with agreed-to incentives to produce and eventually own land from which they would create their own wealth. This system attracted individuals, enterprising and otherwise, from England and provided people on the ground in Virginia a stake in their way of life that proved resilient enough to withstand continued native attacks, political change to being a crown

---

[86] Ibid.

[87] Tony Williams, *The Jamestown Experiment* (Naperville, IL: Sourcebooks, Inc., 2011), 239.

[88] Frank E. Grizzard and Smith, D. Boyd, *Jamestown Colony: A Political, Social, and Cultural History* (Denver: ABC-CLIO Books, 2007), xliv.

colony in 1624, and overcome the threats that nearly caused the new body politic to fold over itself and vanish from history.[89]

Bethell goes so far as to interpret Jamestown with ramifications for international security:

Private property is the most peaceable of institutions, encouraging its owners to cultivate their own gardens and do so productively, rather than to organize into armies and raid the storehouses of neighbors.[90]

Furthermore, this body politic was enduring an ocean away from Europe's throes of the Thirty Year War, where modern notions of sovereignty and security were written into history.

Jamestown provides example for a way of life where the first level of security, individuals in an understood relationship with their direct leviathan, endured. In contrast, for an example of security at the second level, an inadequate leviathan that eventually perished, we turn again to the Congress of Vienna, credited with bringing about the Concert of Europe from 1815 to at least 1848. Kissinger suggests the Congress of Vienna "maintained itself for a hundred years."[91] Actually, the Concert of Europe provides a wonderful example from history where the two levels of security being considered by this paper interacted. At the international level, the agreement among the sovereign states, the system was explicitly a balance of power arrangement with the state as primary referent. As already noted above, some of the more powerful members, such as France and Russia, saw the Congress of Vienna as a charge to conserve this system for all signatories that allowed them reach into the first level of security, the relationship between a state and its individuals. Spain experienced a liberal revolution in 1820 that reinstated its constitution and limited absolute power of the Spanish king.

The Congress of Verona in 1822 called this the Spanish Question. Montmorency, France's Foreign Minister at Verona, argued as a matter of principle and the common interest of Europe to

---

[89] Williams, 256.

[90] Bethell, 36.

[91] Kissinger, 806.

suppress and reverse the Spanish revolution. France sought support to invade and conserve Spain as it had been. Four of the five major powers agreed. France used force, intervened and re-established King Ferdinand VII in 1823.[92] Great Britain disagreed. In addition to the protests cited above, where Lord Castlereagh did not see the Congress of Vienna as "Superintendence of the Internal Affairs of other States," the eminently practical statesman concluded the Spanish question did not constitute a "practical and intelligible Danger, capable of being brought home to the National Feeling," insufficient to justify British military intervention. Castlereagh insisted on the intelligibility of an international problem as a requirement for intervention; that is, action should mean something to the public mind or public sentiment.[93] That is, the Spanish question was not worth the cost of British lives or treasure.

An anecdote that demonstrates how some of the British public mind saw the Spanish question appears in a gilt copper medallion coined to ridicule the political machinations of the Congress of Verona. For the French Minister of War, Chateaubriand, the coin read, "THE KING OF FRANCE MY MASTER DEMANDS THE FREEDOM OF FERDINAND VII TO GIVE HIS PEOPLE INSTITUTIONS THEY CANNOT HOLD BUT FROM HIM." A separate coin for a separate question at Verona shows British scruples about consent of the governed; the coin aimed at Francis I of Austria with the inscription, "MY TROOPS OCCUPY NAPLES TO CHASTISE THE NEAPOLITANS FOR CARING TO CHANGE THEIR CONSTITUTION."[94] Great Britain, arguably the most powerful nation at the time, was unwilling to enforce an international order with states as primary security referent if it meant intervention in another state's inner political process, especially if intervention took from the people what they determined was their "manner of life."

---

[92] W. Alison Phillips, *Modern Europe: 1815-1899* (London: Rivingtons, 1901), 124-6.

[93] Rothschild, 68.

[94] Wikipedia, http://en.wikipedia.org/wiki/Congress_of_Verona (accessed on March 22, 2013).

41

Despite Great Britain's ideological defection from the European system, France's imposition in Spain restored order, at least from a top down perspective. However, the grass roots view, not only in Spain but throughout the continent, reveals murmurings of revolutions. Discontent and the demand for political change spread throughout Europe. W. Alison Phillips recounts

> The thirty years of peace, what at a price the Powers had secured for Europe, had produced their effect…The world, intoxicated with the vision of boundless possibilities of progress, pressed impatiently against the barriers erected by political systems which seemed to it outworn and useless, and therefore intolerable.[95]

Springtime of the Peoples[96] affected every nation in Europe except Great Britain, the Netherlands, Portugal, Russia, and the Ottomans. Notably, in an attempt to counter this revolutionary dynamic and in order to secure Austria as a primary referent in the international order, Tsar Nicolas sent 200,000 Russian troops to compel Hungary to return to the Austrian empire. The Tsar's effort worked superficially and temporarily.[97] The Crimean, Austro Prussian and Prussian Franco Wars punctuated the rest of the century preparing Europe for consummate insecurity, the war to end all wars.

That war did not end all wars; nor did WWII. Lamentably, neither did the Cold War. But it is of use here to examine a significant factor that ended the Cold War: tenets of individual and human rights, precursors to the notion of human security, found in the Helsinki Accords of 1975. What happened there followed the strategic security prescriptions of Wolfers and Kennan cited above. The Western pole used self restraint and satisfied the demands of the other pole, the Soviet Union. Moreover, Helsinki desecuritized freedom of conscience, thought, and religion, in accordance with Ole Weaver's work. In the midst of the Mutually Assured Destruction (MAD) security strategies, Helsinki's two year Conference on Security and Cooperation in Europe agreed

---

[95] Phillips, 237.

[96] See John Merriman, *A History of Modern Europe from the French Revolution to the Present*, cited here to compare with the current phrase "Arab Spring."

[97] Phillips, 248-331.

on ten specific principles which were divided into three baskets. The first and second baskets had to

do with political and economic issues such as respect for the rights of sovereignty, to refrain from

the threat or use of force, inviolability of frontiers, territorial integrity, peaceful resolution of

disputes, and non intervention in internal state affairs.[98]

The Soviet Union perceived the accords as a major diplomatic boost in satisfying its

demands and consolidating Soviet territorial gains in Eastern Europe. President Ford led the West,

and suffered much criticism at the time, as he reaffirmed the U.S. non-recognition policy of the

Baltic States of Estonia, Latvia, and Lithuania. Credited with significantly reducing Cold War

tension, the ten principles (Decalogue) third basekt called for:[99] respect for human rights and

fundamental freedoms (thought, conscience, and religion), equal rights and self determination of

peoples, cooperation among states, and fulfillment in good faith of obligations under international

law.

Helsinki never became a treaty. Nor did it need to: many of the provisions echoed the UN

Charter. Helsinki's Basket III demonstrated a diplomatic push for signatories to consider conditions

in which their citizens lived. Though nations agreed that borders in Europe should be stable, the

Final Agreement recognized frontiers could change by peaceful internal means. Cited as a case

study, the Helsinki Accords provide an example of desecuritizing. Political negotiations minimized

what Soviet bloc elites could securitize. Weaver points out that this led to a speech act failure in

Eastern Europe in 1989. Soviet bloc elites were disabled by non military aspects, human rights, and

Helsinki Basket III principles from credibly employing the speech act of security to use whatever

means they deemed necessary for state survival.[100] Anatoly Dobrynin, the Soviet ambassador to the

---

[98] Kissinger, 759.

[99] Timothy Sowula, "The Helsinki Process and the Death of Communism," *Open Democracy* (July 2005): http://www.opendemocracy.net/democracy-protest/helsinki_2716.jsp (accessed on January 30, 2013).

[100] Weaver, 60.

United States from 1962 to 1986, described Helsinki as a legal and moral trap.[101] Kissinger

attributes success to human rights activists and recognizes the heroism of Vaclav Havel and Lech

Walesa as they used Basket III provisions to domestically and internationally undermine not only

Soviet domination but communist regimes in their own countries.[102] Kissinger remembers having to

defend U.S. actions at Helsinki amidst severe criticism. He delivered a speech three weeks after the

conference:

> At Helsinki, for the first time in the postwar period, human rights and fundamental
> freedoms became recognized subjects of East-West discourse and negotiation. The
> conference put forward *our* standards of humane conduct, which have been—and still are—
> a beacon of hope to millions.[103]

In this instance, history showed that how a government treats millions of individuals matters. The

United States emerged as the main superpower from the Cold War.

John Ikenberry considers the current world order in his 2011 book, *Liberal Leviathan*. In it,

he asserts during the Cold War the United States led a liberal hegemonic order, organized around

multilateral institutions, alliances, special relationships and client states and defined in terms of

provision of security, wealth creation, and social advancement. Ikenberry deems it the most

successful order in world history. He continues by recognizing a current crisis of authority in this

American led liberal world order. The rise of unipolarity, eroded norms of state sovereignty,

shifting sources of violence, and intensifying security interdependence make liberal hegemony

more problematic. Rather than destroying the order, Ikenberry sees a new kind of liberal

international order emerging, one that is more inclusive, less hierarchical, permeated with

unfamiliar forms of cooperation. He prescribes the United States renegotiate hegemonic bargains

with other states, recapture the public philosophy of liberal internationalism, which blends liberal

---

[101] John Lewis Gaddis, *The Cold War: A New History* (New York: The Penguin Press, 2005), 190.

[102] Kissinger, 759.

[103] Ibid., 760.

and realist thinking, and "lead through rules," saying power is most durable and legitimate when exercised in a system of rules.[104]

Kissinger sees the post Cold War world in this way.

> The issue is whether the post-Cold War world can find some principle to restrain the assertion of power and self-interest. Of course, in the end a balance of power always comes about *de facto* when several states interact. The question is whether the maintenance of the international system can turn into a conscious design, or whether it will grow out of a series of tests of strength.[105]

Ikenberry sees power balance developing in response to U.S. unipolarity because the disappearance of the Cold War threat removes leverage for the unipolar state; he cites Gaddis, the "something worse [over the horizon]" disappears.[106] The question for Ikenberry, in contrast to Kissinger, revolves around whether the United States will act as an imperial leviathan or a liberal leviathan.[107]

So, what has the United States been doing with its power? How has it been behaving in terms of security? In terms of world order? President Clinton sent a message in 1999.

> [W]e can say to the people of the world, whether you live in Africa, or Central Europe, or any other place, if somebody comes after innocent civilians and tries to kill them en masse because of their race, their ethnic background or their religion, and it's within our power to stop it, we will stop it.[108]

---

[104] John G. Ikenberry, *Liberal Leviathan: The Origins, Crisis, and Transformation of the American World Order* (Princeton: Princeton University Press, 2011), xi-xv.

[105] Kissinger, 77.

[106] Ikenberry, 241-246.

[107] Ibid., 28.

[108] See a paper delivered by Rodger A. Payne from the University of Louisville, "Human Security and American Foreign Policy," at a conference for Human Security in the New Millenium at the University of Missouri in Columbia, MO, March of 2004, http://www.academia.edu/554001/_Human_Security_and_American_Foreign_Policy_ (accessed on March 3, 2013):10.

Though Secretary of State Madeleine Albright backpedaled from this remark,[109] U.S. and NATO actions in Kosovo demonstrate the Clinton Doctrine in the sole superpower world.

In contrast to Clinton, Ikenberry suggests that the Bush administration behaved in important respects as a hegemon with imperial characteristics, providing rule and order based on its unilateral assertion of power and rights.[110] "At the heart of the Bush Doctrine was the proposition that the [U.S.] would act directly—and alone, if necessary—in pursuit of global security threats that it identified, and in this struggle countries were either with the [U.S.] or against it."[111] Ikenberry, citing the Iraq experience, asserts that the U.S. has failed as a conservative and imperial Leviathan, "the world has rejected it, and the [U.S.] cannot sustain it."[112]

Just as the security environment is changing, the notion of sovereignty is losing its semi sacrosanct power with implications for U.S. and liberal behavior. Kofi Annan observed in 1999.

> State sovereignty, in its most basic sense, is being redefined. [Modern states are] now widely understood to be instruments at the service of their people, and not vice versa…When we read the Charter today, we are more than ever conscious of that its aim is to protect individual human rights, not to protect those who abuse them.[113]

The case of Libyan intervention in 2011 provides an example of just this. President Obama explained U.S. and NATO intervention,

> To brush aside America's responsibility as a leader and - more profoundly - our responsibilities to our fellow human beings under such circumstances would have been a betrayal of who we are…In this particular nation, at this particular moment, we were faced with the prospect of violence on an horrific scale.[114]

---

[109] Ibid.

[110] Ikenberry, 30.

[111] Ibid., 255.

[112] Ibid., 30.

[113] Ibid., 248.

[114] President Obama, "Obama Libya Speech Strongly Defends Intervention," http://www.huffingtonpost.com/2011/03/28/obama-libya-speech-_n_841311.html (accessed on March 26, 2013).

The initial coalition of 10 states, certain members of NATO and Qatar, militarily operated

to impose a no-fly zone in accordance with UN Security Council Resolution 1973 and acted under

the authority of Chapter VII of the UN Charter. That coalition grew to nineteen states in the course

of the operations from March through October of that year. Nations involved named their action

Operation Unified Protector. A principal author of the Right to Protect, adopted at the 2005 UN

World Summit, Gareth Evans described the action as "not about bombing for democracy or

Muammar Qaddafi's head. Legally, morally, politically, and militarily it has only one justification:

protecting the country's people."[115] Among the nations involved, the United Kingdom spent an

estimate of up to US$ 1.5 billion, the United States up to US$ 1.1 billion, and Italy up to US$ 750

million as the top three; the top ten spending nations were all Western.[116] This is an example of a

coalition coalescing around human security principles of protection against violence, in accordance

with MacFarlane's and Khoong's recommendations. One could also see it as an international liberal

leviathan enforcing people protection. Ikenberry believes the United States performs better as a

liberal leviathan and recommends that the United States should seek to consolidate a global order

where other countries "bandwagon" rather than balance against it.[117] The Libya case appears as

such an example.

The final case study considers U.S. action to counter the Lord's Resistance Army (LRA). In

October of 2011, the United States sent 100 armed military advisors, largely believed to be special

operations troops, to support the efforts of four central African nations in countering the LRA.

Under the leadership of Joseph Kony, indicted by the International Criminal Court in 2005, the

LRA has killed, raped, maimed, and kidnapped with impunity since the 1980s in Uganda, Central

---

[115] Council on Foreign Relations "Libya and the Responsibility to Protect," 24 March 2011, http://www.webcitation.org/5xsX2ZLd2 (accessed on March 3, 2013).

[116] See the Wikipedia article, http://en.wikipedia.org/wiki/2011_military_intervention_in_Libya

[117] Ikenberry, 32.

African Republic, Democratic Republic of Congo and South Sudan.[118] In addition to the military

advisors, the State Department has at least two officials deployed to Uganda. The President's

strategy intends to forge regional consensus and action and enable the local governments to protect

their people,[119] a basic charge to the first level leviathan. In January, Congress passed a bipartisan

bill, Rewards for Justice, that in effect put a US$ 5 million bounty on Kony's head; the U.S. State

Department has a website where anonymous information can be submitted.[120] This counter LRA

mission has enjoyed recent successes: LRA killings have dropped 67% since from 2011 to 2012,

two high ranking LRA commanders have been caught, defections of higher and lower level

members has increased to record levels.[121] In a separate but related event, a Congolese warlord,

Bosco Ntaganda, turned himself into the U.S. Embassy in Rwanda to be transferred to the ICC.[122]

CONCLUSION

Because of its security tradition of a protective relationship between state and individual,

the United States and liberal coalitions are acting to protect people from organized violence,

behaving as a *de facto* global leviathan in support of that aspect of the UN's human security when

interests and circumstances permit. However, this permissive international environment exists in a

unipolar world. As the world becomes multipolar, will the West be restrained from behaving as a

---

[118] Thom Shanker and Rick Gladstone, "Armed U.S. Advisors to Help Fight Renegade Group," *New York Times*, http://www.nytimes.com/2011/10/15/world/africa/barack-obama-sending-100-armed-advisers-to-africa-to-help-fight-lords-resistance-army.html?_r=0 (accessed on 26 March 2013).

[119] Jon Gandomi, U.S. embassy official, email message to author. February 25, 2013.

[120] See https://www.rewardsforjustice.net/index.cfm?page=tip&language=english

[121] Perry Chiaramonte, Invisible Children soldiers on with KONY 2012 campaign as warlord is in hiding, http://www.foxnews.com/world/2013/03/24/invisible-children-soldiers-on-with-kony-2012-campaign-as-warlord-is-in-hiding/ (accessed on April 6, 2013).

[122] Mike Pflanz, "Terminator Bosco Ntaganda Heads to ICC," *The Telegraph*, http://www.telegraph.co.uk/news/worldnews/africaandindianocean/democraticrepublicofcongo/9948750/Terminator-Bosco-Ntaganda-heads-to-ICC.html (accessed on 26 March 2013).

leviathan to protect people in accordance with liberal traditions? If the West is restrained, will it be supplanted by a different leviathan? Other rising national powers do not have liberal traditions and are likely to check U.S. and Western action. Consider Syria. Russia and China have vetoed UN Security Council sanctions against Syria where the UN estimates over 70,000 people have been killed.[123] Russia continues to warn against any type of military intervention.[124] Is Syria but the first instance when the West will be stopped from behaving as the international leviathan?

Kosovo, Libya, the counter LRA mission, and recent developments in Mali demonstrate liberal leviathan behavior. Furthermore, on March 28, 2013, the UN Security Council, in a resolution sponsored by the United States, France, and Togo, authorized an intervention brigade to take military action against rebels "to decisively counter the destructive violence" in eastern Democratic Republic of Congo (DRC). There will be three infantry battalions, an artillery company and one each of special forces and reconnaissance companies. This is the first time in history the UN has issued an offensive mandate to take military action against rebels.[125] Ironic that the last quote about DRC intervention came from the Russian ambassador to the UN, who holds the current Security Council presidency, and supported the DRC resolution.

This paper has focused on Western liberal security perspectives. The world is becoming more multipolar as other national powers such as Brazil, Russia, India, China, and South Africa, the association of emerging economies known as BRICS, assert their presence on the world stage. How do some of these rising powers see international relations theory? Buzan and Acharya compiled a

---

[123] Joe Lauria, "Russia, China Veto Syria Resolution at U.N.," *The Wall Street Journal*, http://online.wsj.com/article/SB10000872396390444097904577536793560681930.html, (accessed on March 3, 2013).

[124] Dominic Evans, "Russia warns West over Syria after Obama threats," *Reuters*, http://www.reuters.com/article/2012/08/21/us-syria-crisis-idUSBRE8610SH20120821, (accessed on March 3, 2013).

[125] Edith M. Lederer, "UN Authorizes Intervention Force for Congo," ABC News, http://abcnews.go.com/US/wireStory/set-authorize-intervention-force-congo-18832597#.UVTA-WncgWo (accessed on March 28, 2013).

book which queried Eastern intellectuals, "Why is there no non-Western international relations

theory?" Among the answers, China's three guiding principles are *tianxia*, a Confucian tributary

system, *datong*, or great harmony, and order. Though it literally means "space under heaven,"

tianxia implies inequality but in a sense that is difficult for Westerners to understand. It intends a

holist approach that never has something opposite or intolerant or that requires conflict to solve.

Tianxia takes care of the whole world, aiming at a harmonious whole, when combined with *datong*.

Thirdly, order is the most important principle in Confucian thought. Qin observes

> …[*tianxia*] in the eye of a Confucian scholar was not that between the animals in a
> Hobbesian jungle, equal and hostile; not that between the humans in Lockean
> society, equal and competitive; not even that between the states in the Kantian
> culture, equal and friendly. Rather, it was…unequal but benign…it does not
> assume a jungle but a society.[126]

How, then, does China understand security, make policy, and act on it in the national

sense? China's new president, Xi Jinping, just stated, "that the world shouldn't become 'an arena

where gladiators fight each other…Rather than undercutting each other's efforts, countries should

complement each other and work for joint progress.'" At the same time, without reference to a

specific nation, Mr. Xi suggested that no one should be allowed to throw a region and even the

whole world into chaos for selfish gains."[127] Perhaps Mr. Xi was speaking of North Korea.

However, if China feels that the U.S. is attempting to contain China's strategic rise "for selfish

gain," how will this situation man ifest?

South of China, India's response to the Acharya and Buzan prompt highlights Western

duality as a basis for the "fear the other" which dominates Western international relations, i.e.

security. Behera diagnoses this as a significant source of conflict.

---

[126] Yaqing Qin, "Why is there no Chinese international relations theory?" in *Non Western International Relations Theory: Perspectives on and beyond Asia,* ed Amitav Acharya and Barry Buzan (New York: Routledge, Taylor and Francis Group, 2010), 41-43.

[127] Andrew Browne, "China's Xi sets tone on regional relations," *Wall Street Journal,* http://online.wsj.com/article/SB10001424127887323550604578408092342369184.html (accessed on April 7, 2013).

Internationally, there are divisive ramifications of externalizing the *other* in constructing a nationalist identity, which generates hatred for an alien community or foreign country…true for…India and Pakistan whose enmity is historically cast in their conflicting religious ideologies… [while] the sole superpower—the US—whose perennial search for an 'enemy', met the *other* in the…evil empire of the Soviet Union…Cuba, Iran, Libya, and Iraq were labeled as the 'rogue states' and the ongoing 'war on terror' targets the 'axis of evil'…a non-dualistic mode of thinking that does not generate a 'fear of the other' has far reaching implications for contemporary international politics.[128]

Behera's prescription is to do away with 'self-other' binary mode view though he acknowledges, in the end, this is an uncharted but promising path.[129] India's and China's views represent two rising powers, how they understand international relations and how it is different from the West.

In a separate but related vein, because security has to do with national character and policy, Bhutan has a Gross National Happiness (GNH) index. Bhutan measures its GNH with a sophisticated survey instrument and incorporates results in its five year process that guides national economic and development planning. A Western economist decries such an instrument as "unscientific" as it will only tell you how people use words.[130] However, in an effort to see where the twain of East and West have met when hearing about Bhutan's GNH, one cannot ignore Bentham's felicific calculus approach to policy and Jefferson's inclusion of the word "happiness" in the Declaration of Independence. At the same time, it is not difficult to imagine a northern Montana woodsman, whose history of rugged individualism has made his life, asking, "Is it the government's role to deliver happiness to people?"

Happiness and Montana woodsmen aside, this paper is about security. If the West can no longer act as an international leviathan, it is unlikely that a different leviathan with the global reach,

---

[128] Navnita Chadha Behera, "Re-imagining IR in India," in *Non-Western International Relations Theory* (New York: Routledge, Taylor and Francis Group, 2010), 111.

[129] Ibid.

[130] Deirdre N. McCloskey, "Happyism: The Creepy New Economics of Pleasure," *The New Republic* (June 28, 2012): 16–23, http://www.newrepublic.com/article/politics/magazine/103952/happyism-deirdre-mccloskey-economics-happiness# (accessed on April 7, 2013).

scale, and scope could take its place in the near to medium term. This paper assumes, because it is a product of Western thought, that a leviathan is necessary for security, for people to enjoy what they value and create. Can the UN ever be *de facto* and *de jure* leviathan for human security? Are these next ten years a perishing opportunity for the United States and like minded nations to act as a *de facto* global leviathan on behalf of liberal values? What will the United States do in the name of security as its power decreases in proportion to other nations? Admiral James Crowe, former Chairman of the Joints Chiefs of Staff, speaking about terrorists but extensible to any named security threat offered guidance after September 11, 2001. "The real danger lies with not what the terrorists can do to us but what we can do to ourselves when we are spooked."[131] This paper asks two final questions about humans and security. If security concerns individuals and their manner of life brought about by submitting to common political bonds, whether those bonds be Western liberal or Eastern holistic, how can nations working together create space on this earth in which we, the peoples, can at least avoid the evil of insecurity, war? Or is war an inherent part of security, the *yin* and *yang* of the world, when different manners of life, different human systems operate so closely together?

---

[131] Stephen Flynn, *The Edge of Disaster: Rebuilding a Resilient Nation* (New York: Random House, 2007), 93.

BIBLIOGRAPHY

Achrya, Amitav and Barry Buzan, eds. *Non-Western International Relations Theory*. New York: Routledge, Taylor and Francis Group, 2010.

Bacevich, Andrew J. *American Empire*. Cambridge: Harvard University Press, 2002.

Bacevich, Andrew J., ed. *The Long War*. New York: Columbia University Press, 2007.

Barro, R. J. and McCleary, R. M. *Which Countries Have State Religions?* Illinois: University of Chicago Press, 2006.

Bethell, Tom. *The Noblest Triumph: Property and Prosperity through the Ages*. New York: St. Martin's Press, 1998.

Buzan, Barry. *People, States, and Fear: An Agenda for International Security Studies in the Post Cold War Era, 2nd ed.* Boulder: Lynne Rienner Publishers, 2008.

Clausewitz, Carl Von. *On War*, ed and trans. by Michael Howard and Peter Paret. Princeton: Princeton University Press, 1984.

Fischer, David Hackett. *Washington's Crossing*. New York: Oxford University Press, 2004.

Flynn, Stephen. *The Edge of Disaster: Rebuilding a Resilient Nation*. New York: Random House, 2007.

Friedman, Thomas H. *The World is Flat*. New York: Farrar, Straus and Giroux, 2005.

Gaddis, John Lewis. *The Cold War: A New History*. New York: The Penguin Press, 2005.

_____. *George F. Kennan: An American Life*. New York: Penguin Press, 2011.

Grizzard, Frank E. and Boyd D. Smith. *Jamestown Colony: A Political, Social, and Cultural History*. California: ABC-CLIO, Inc., 2007.

Hobbes, Thomas. *Leviathan or the Matter, Forme, & Power of a Commonwealth, Ecclesiastical and Civill*. Printed for Andrew Crooke at the Green Dragon in St. Paul's Churchyard, 1651.

Ikenberry, G. John. *Liberal Leviathan: The Origins, Crisis, and Transformation of the American World Order*. Princeton: Princeton University Press, 2011.

Jones, James L., "Message to the Next Administration: An Unasked for Response," Address to the Business Executives for National Security dinner, Kansas City, MO, September 6, 2012.

Kennan, George F. Telegram 511. http://www.gwu.edu/~nsarchiv/coldwar/documents/episode-1/kennan.htm, accessed on 21 March 2013.

Kennan, George F. "Soviet Sources of Conduct." *Foreign Affairs* (August 1947): http://www.historyguide.org/europe/kennan.html, accessed on 21 March 2013.

Kissinger, Henry. *Diplomacy*. New York: Simon & Schuster, 1994.

Lipschutz, Ronnie D., ed. *On Security*. New York: Columbia University Press, 1995.

MacFarlane, S. Neil and Yuen Foong Khong. *Human Security and the UN: A Critical History.* Bloomington: Indiana University Press, 2006.

Mason, Adolphus T. *Free Government in the Making*, 3rd ed. New York: Oxford University Press, 1965.

Merriman, John. *A History of Modern Europe from the French Revolution to the Present.* New York: W. W. Norton & Company, 2010.

Rothschild, Emma. "What is Security?" *Daedalus*, 124, no. 3 (Summer 1995): 53.

Strassler, Robert B. *The Landmark Thucydides: A Comprehensive Guide to the Peloponnesian War.* New York: Simon and Schuster, 1998.

Timothy Sowula. "*The Helsinki Process and the Death of Communism.*" Open Democracy (July 2005): http://www.opendemocracy.net/democracy-protest/helsinki_2716.jsp (accessed on 30 January 2013).

Turabian, Kate L. *A Manual for Writers of Research Papers, Theses, and Dissertations.* 7th ed. Chicago: University of Chicago Press, 2007.

Williams, Tony. *The Jamestown Experiment*. Naperville, IL: Sourcebooks, Inc., 2011.

Stone, Marianne. "Security According to Buzan: A Comprehensive Security Analysis." *Security Discussion Papers Series 1* Grooupe d'Etudes et d'Expertise "Securité et Technologies" GEEST-2009 (Spring 2009).

Ullman, Richard H. "Redefining Security." *International Security*, Vol. 8, No. 1 (Summer 1983): 129-153.

United Nations, *Concepts of Security*. New York, 1986.

Wilson, Woodrow. *An Address to Senate* on January 22, 1917. http://www.firstworldwar.com/source/peacewithoutvictory.htm (accessed on 24 February 2013).